The Jungle Radio

Bird Songs *of* India

written and illustrated by
Devangana Dash

...ouse

PUFFIN BOOKS

USA | Canada | UK | Ireland | Australia
New Zealand | India | South Africa | China

Puffin Books is part of the Penguin Random House group of companies
whose addresses can be found at global.penguinrandomhouse.com

Published by Penguin Random House India Pvt. Ltd
7th Floor, Infinity Tower C, DLF Cyber City,
Gurgaon 122 002, Haryana, India

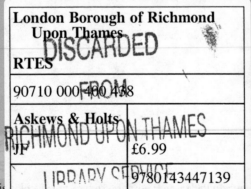

Penguin
Random House
India

First published in Puffin Books by Penguin Random House India 2019

Copyright © Devangana Dash 2019

10 9 8 7 6 5 4 3 2 1

ISBN 9780143447139

Typeset in Varius 1 LT Std, Smile ICG and Adobe Garamond Pro
Printed at Replika Press Pvt. Ltd, India

www.penguin.co.in

READING the RADIO

Birds love to sing. The most musical of creatures, they have their own reasons to do so. It can be to call out and attract a loved one or to announce a new home. They call when they are alarmed, or simply because they want to sing—alone, in duets or in groups. And some even mimic other sounds they find around them.

Bird sounds are everywhere in nature—making music in the sky, in trees and in our rivers. To me, this rich choir is just like the radio—with the constant chattering and singing. If you listen carefully, you can find this radio in a jungle, a bird or national sanctuary, in a park near you or your own balcony at home!

The pages that follow comprise a playlist of the songs of thirty Indian birds. A girl named Gul will take you along and help you discover birds—a familiar few, and others that are new. Go to the end of the story to know the full names of the ones you like, and the next time you visit a national park, a jungle or a beach, I hope you spot your new feathered friends. To identify the sounds of these colourful birds, all you have to do is look out for the big colourful letters. You can read them with Gul, but if you stand up and sing them aloud, it's even better!

Okay, now, tuning in
in kee . . . koo . . . one . . . go!

Early one morning
in the jolly month of June,
Gul sat in her veranda,
swaying gently to her own tune

Suddenly her radio chanted,
chak-chip-chippurrr chham chham,
strange sounds and jingles
she found difficult to hum

Moving closer,
she was curious to know,
'who are the musicians
of this sweet-sounding radio show?'

In the blink of an eye,
the radio sent her off to find musical clues,
to the land of countless colours—
yellows, oranges, lush greens and blues

Birds—one hundred, maybe two,
many out of sight,
singing sunny tunes at their loudest
at the day's first light

She listened to the sounds
filling the silence of dawn—
a growl, cheer, howl . . .
or was it a screech, or a yawn?

Baffled, Gul asked aloud,
'who is it that speaks,
songs and melodies
from those murmuring beaks?'

She spotted someone familiar—
a Magpie, singing with glee,

in a chirpy

CHURR-CHOOO

and a sweet

SWEE-WEE-WEE

To her left, three friends she met,
singing in a honey-coated voice—
a Babbler, Fairy and Thrush,
whistling tunes of their choice

TEW-TOO-TOOO
TEW-TOO-TOOO

Pitched in the Shama on the side,
humming his flute-like melody with pride

Lured by the music,
Gul exclaimed, 'wow!'
when someone repeated after her,
she inquired, 'who is it that speaks now?'

A KEE-KEE,
KOO-KOOO...
another
what Gul spoke,
a Drongo uttered it too!

A Coucal entering the mimic's show
was surprised on hearing his own call—
a loud goop on a loop—
for whatever the Drongo heard, he stole it all

GOOOOP
GOOP
GOOP
GOOOOOP

Five noisy Parakeets
chuckled at this episode
and laughed with a rowdy

KreaK
 KreAK
KkrrrrEeAKkkK...

Joined by a Woodpecker
tap tapp tappp-ing a trunk
like a drum with his beak

TAP

TAPP

TAPP

Listening to the lyrical songs,
Gul wished to sing too,

so she raised an alarm with the Pitta bird
with a ringing wheet-tew on cue

WHEE-TEWW

WHEEEE-TEW

WHEEE-TEWWW

Ruffling his feathers,
a Hoopoe, who wanted to join this game,
flicked his fan and shook his crown
and called out his own name!

HOOP POO POO

HOOP POOO POO

A Sunbird and a Flycatcher,
along with two White-Eyes in a tree,
chirped chee chee chee-erfully
with their soft nasal notes

CHUCKK-CHIPPP
CHUCKK-CHREE

More birds surprised Gul,
as, collecting sounds, she walked,
not among singers this time,
but birds who talked!

'BRAIN-FEVERRR!' said the Cuckoo,
repeating it after a pause,

chiming in with a 'DID HE DO IT' call
a little Lapwing there was

A Tailorbird, squawking
and busy stitching his nest,
more heard than seen,
he was hidden from the rest

TOWIT—TOWIT T—TOWI T

A lonely Barbet
finishing his meal of the day
called out in a repetitive roar,
asking the Tailor to play

KUT

KUT

KUT T

KUTROOOO

Then, like thunder,
a Roller dived in the air
with a burst of blue sparkles . . .

Troubling the shy Moorhen
with rasping CROAKS
and CACKLES

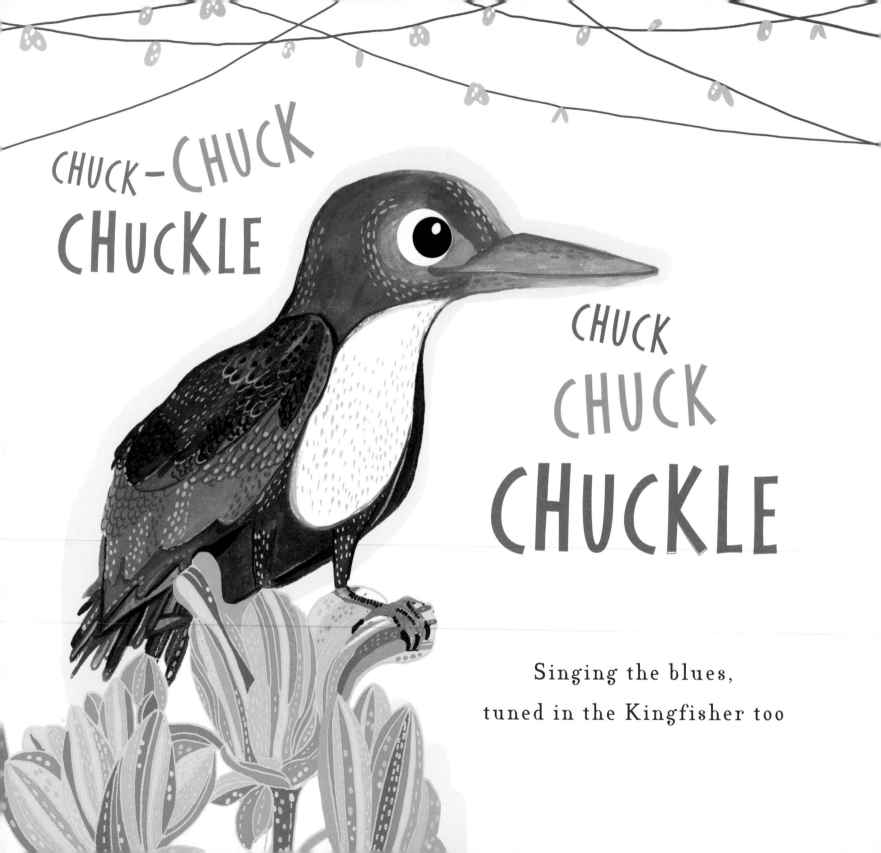

CHUCK-CHUCK
CHUCKLE

CHUCK
CHUCK
CHUCKLE

Singing the blues,
tuned in the Kingfisher too

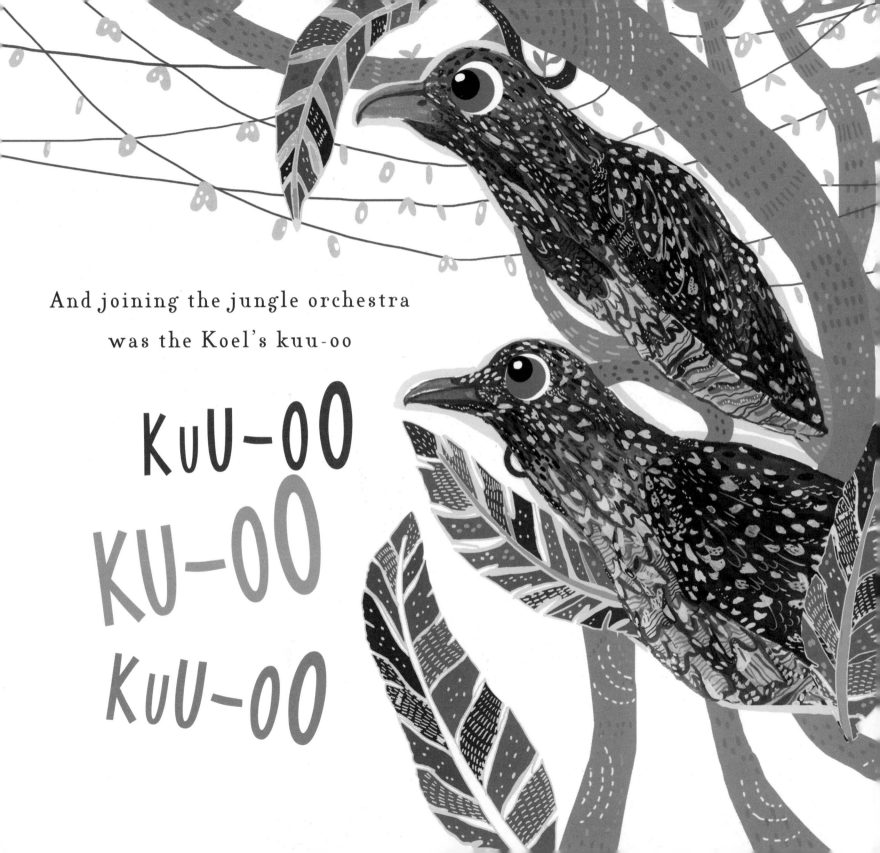

And joining the jungle orchestra
was the Koel's kuu-oo

KuU-oo
KU-oo
KuU-oo

The Seven Sisters
were distressed,
in a giant tree that
wouldn't stand still . . .

CHI-CHII-CHI-
KIki-KIKiki
CHI-CHII

CHI
CHI
CHI
CHI

By the harsh

TR-TRR-TRR

TRUMPPET

of the
Malabar Hornbill

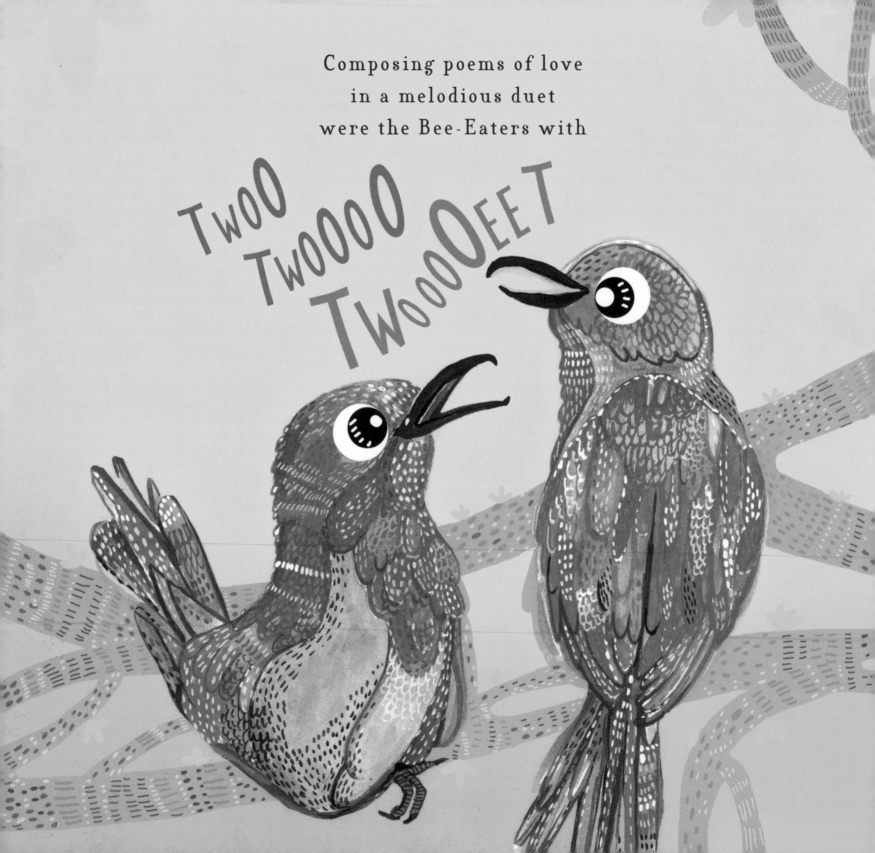

Composing poems of love
in a melodious duet
were the Bee-Eaters with

TwooO TwoOooO TwoOOeeT
TwoOOOeeT

Raiding their peace were the Treepies,
flap-flap-flapping their wings

with
KaK-KaK
and
Ko-TReEE,
mocking anyone who sings

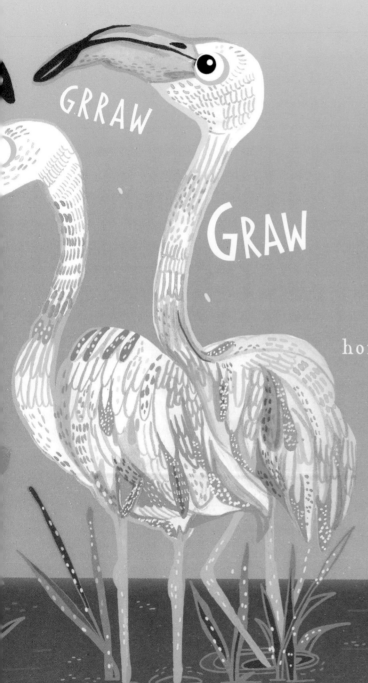

GRRAW

GRAW

Tall pink Flamingoes in a flock
were engrossed in their chatter,
with their twisty coat-hanger necks
honking all the jungle news in non-stop jabber

Then Gul saw a bird named Paradise,
who had a wheezing whine and wail
waking from a bad dream, bouncing
and waving his long feathery ribbon-tail

CHEE-CHEEW
CHE-
CHEEW

The meandering Munias,
blushing like fresh berries,
tweeted their soft song
to drive away his worries

Treasuring the spirited songs
that Gul had gathered today,
she made her way home at dusk
as the songs faded away

The Nightjar sang her a lullaby,
resting on the ground,
clicking and churrringgg
like a skipping stone's sound

CHIT-CHIT-CHITRR
CHITRROoOOoRRR-ORRRRRR

Switching off her radio,
Gul tucked herself in bed,
to dream of her feathered friends,
the rhythms, the songs and the ones that lay ahead

If you listen carefully tonight
to the musical land beyond your wall,
you'll hear the jungle singing for you,
'goodnight, Gul . . . goodnight, all!'

WHAT'S THAT BIRD?

 Oriental Magpie-Robin

 Indian Scimitar-Babbler

 Asian Fairy-Bluebird

 Malabar Whistling-Thrush

 White-Rumped Shama

 Black Drongo

 Greater Coucal

 Malabar Parakeet

 Black-Rumped Flameback

 Oriental White-Eye

 Nilgiri Flycatcher

 Small Sunbird

 Indian Pitta

 Hoopoe

 Red-Wattled Lapwing

 Common Hawk-Cuckoo (Brainfever Bird)

 Common Tailorbird

 Brown-Headed Barbet

 Indian Roller

 Purple Moorhen

 White-Breasted Kingfisher

 Asian Koel

 Jungle Babbler (Seven Sisters)

 Malabar Hornbill

 Blue-Bearded Bee-Eater

 Rufous Treepie

 Greater Flamingo

 Asian Paradise Flycatcher

 Red Munia

 Common Indian Nightjar

BIRD SANCTUARIES IN INDIA

Sultanpur Bird Sanctuary (Haryana)

Okhla Bird Sanctuary (Uttar Pradesh)

Chilika Lake Bird Sanctuary (Odisha)

Salim Ali Bird Sanctuary (Goa)

Keoladeo Bird Sanctuary (Rajasthan)

Ranganathittu Bird Sanctuary (Karnataka)

Kutch Bustard and **Nal Sarovar** bird sanctuaries (Gujarat)

Mayani and **Bhigwan** bird sanctuaries (Maharashtra)

Kumarakom and **Thattekad** bird sanctuaries (Kerala)

Eaglenest Wildlife Sanctuary (Arunachal Pradesh)

Pulicat Lake Bird Sanctuary and

Kaundinya Wildlife Sanctuary (Andhra Pradesh)

Vedanthangal Bird Sanctuary (Tamil Nadu)

BIRDING BY EAR

Song Birds of India (www.birdcalls.info)

The Cornell Lab of Ornithology (www.birds.cornell.edu)

Xeno-Canto: Sharing Bird Sounds from around the World (www.xeno-canto.org)

Listening Earth: Soundscapes of our Natural World (www.listeningearth.com)

The Internet Bird Collection (www.hbw.com/ibc)

Birds-of-Paradise Project (www.birdsofparadiseproject.org)

Birdsong.fm (www.birdsong.fm)

Wild Sanctuary (www.wildsanctuary.com)

Smithsonian's Migratory Bird Centre (nationalzoo.si.edu/migratory-birds)

ON YOUR NEXT BIRDING ADVENTURE...

• You'll need a pair of binoculars and a sun hat.

• Keep a field guide with information and pictures of the birds found in that area. You can also carry a weatherproof notebook and put down the names of the birds you see, the sounds they make and what they get up to. This can be your own bird book!

• Try and go with a birdwatching group or take the help of a birdwatcher.

• Respect the birds and their natural habitat, and avoid wearing very bright clothes or using flash photography.

• Listen as closely as you can.

• Learn bird-directions to spot more birds. It helps to imagine the hands of a clock—12 o'clock is up ahead, 3 o'clock is right, 6 o'clock is behind and 9 o'clock is to the left.

• Don't just look up—some birds perch on the ground too! So make sure you scan the ground.

• Early morning is the best time for birdwatching since that's when birds are most active and tend to call more often.

HAPPY BIRDING!

DEVANGANA DASH is a New Delhi-based designer, illustrator and book maker. When she's not designing books for a living, she reads, draws a little more and collects books for her dream library. For inspiration, she relies on nature (especially birds and sea turtles), picture books by her favourite artists and authors, different genres of music and a cup of chai.

She studied visual communication design at Srishti School of Art, Design and Technology after completing a bachelor's degree in sociology from Lady Shri Ram College for Women. This is Devangana's debut picture book, and she has previously worked with clients like Child Rights and You, WWF India, the Wildlife Trust of India and the Centre of Environment Education. She has also illustrated *Ayesha and the Firefish* (published by Puffin Books in 2016). She can be found on devanganadash.com and on Instagram @devanganadash.

Thank you!

Smit Zaveri, my brilliant editor and the calm behind the chaos. Her enthusiasm, attention to detail, patience and just plain excellence in what she does made this radio sing its song!

My mentors **Srivi Kalyan**, **Kavita Arvind** and **Meera Curam**, who brought me close to the world of birdwatching as well as illustrating and writing for children. **Anupama Arun**, for her infectious enthusiasm for all things natural and wild and for the most inspiring walks in Bandipur and Goa. **Rustam Vania**, for being patient with my bag of questions and self-doubt. For his constant reminders to never stop writing, and for the fish curry and rice.

Geetha Narayanan, director, Srishti School of Art, Design and Technology—the school that taught me everything I do with love today. The **Wildlife Trust of India**, with whose support this book was conceptualized and written.

The kind first few readers of this book for their encouragement—**Sanjeev Sanyal**, **Roopa Pai**, **Deepak Dalal** and **Nayanika Mahtani**. **Ranjit Lal**, for inspiring me with his own work and bettering mine.

My dear sister, **Vasundhara**, for making me brave in the wild. My loving **parents** for their unwavering faith and for making everything possible.

Nimmy Chacko, friend and terrific editor, for believing in this book before anyone else did. **Abismrita Chakravarty**, for existing, listening and always saying what I need to hear.

Ahlawat Gunjan for his constant support and encouragement. **Neelima P Aryan** for her kindness through my panic attacks. **Kankana Basu** for being thorough with the copy-edits. **Parul Kaushik** for letting me get lost in 'The Chocolate Factory' when I needed some respite from reality.

My colleagues at **Penguin Random House India**, residence of the best makers of books in the industry—a place where I have learnt so much.

The places that captivated the birdwatcher in me and inspired me to write this book—**Bandipur Tiger Reserve and National Park** (Karnataka), **Salim Ali Bird Sanctuary** (Goa) and **Manglajodi Ecotourism** (Odisha). The Birdman of India, the late **Salim Ali**, whose writings formed the foundation of this book. Lastly, all the birders I have met so far and from whom I have learnt something new every single time.